Amaryllis
Pride and Determination

Anemone
Anticipation and Protection

Azalea
Temperance and Abundance

Camellia
Gratitude and Admiration

Carnation
Love and Admiration

Chrysanthemum
Loyalty and Honesty

Daffodil
New Beginnings and Happiness

Forget-Me-Not
True Love and Remembrance

Gladiolus
Strength of Character

Iris
Wisdom and Courage

Lavender
Devotion and Calmness

Lily
Purity and Enlightenment

Lily of the Valley
Happiness and Humility

Marigold
Desire for Wealth and Success

Orchid
Elegance and Refinement

Peony
Good Fortune and Prosperity

Rose
Love, Passion, and Beauty

Sunflower
Adoration and Loyalty

Tulip
Perfect Love and Fame

Violet
Modesty and Humility

Zinnia
Thoughts of Absent Friends

Made in the USA
Columbia, SC
23 December 2023

28540735R00028